WOODSMOKE, WIND, AND THE PEREGRINE

Woodsmoke, Wind, and the Peregrine

Shaun T. Griffin

Virginia City NV
10/14/11
For Carolyn —
dear friend,
fellow traveler
on the long
road —
w/ love

Rainshadow Editions
Black Rock Press
University of Nevada, Reno
2008

ISBN 978-1-891033-38-4

Library of Congress Control Number:
2008927260

Printed in the United States of America

The Black Rock Press
University of Nevada, Reno
Reno, NV 89557-0044
www.blackrockpress.org

Cover art by Ismael García Santillanes

Sumi ink text drawings by Shaun T. Griffin

Contents

Acknowledgments

My deep thanks to Ismael García Santillanes—dear friend, painter, and poet—for his watercolor painting on the cover of this book.

The author is grateful for permission to reprint "Osprey on the Deschutes," in the *90 Poets of the Nineties* anthology, 1998; "Winter Admonitions, Christmas Day, Skiing Mount Rose," in *Calapooya*; "First Light, Collioure," and (in slightly different form) "Woodsmoke, Wind, and the Peregrine," in *The MacGuffin*; "Postcard to Wally Easterly from Here in the Loneliest Town on Highway 50," and "Releasing Sparrows at the Buddhist Temple," in *Red Rock Review*; "This Is Not Love's Offering," in the *Poetry Daily* anthology, 2003; "Emerald Lake," in *Southern Humanities Review*; "The Snowy Egret Slough," "Hummingbird," and "The Loons on Walker Lake" in *Elsewhere*; to Robert L. Reid for his quote from *Mountains of the Great Blue Dream* which appeared in "The Last Songbird on Malta," in *Weber Studies*; to e. e. cummings for his quote from "in Just-" in *100 Selected Poems* which appeared in "The Grey Elliot Riff"; and to Hayden Carruth for his quote from "40" in *The Sleeping Beauty* which appeared in "Waking from the Charcoal Dark."

"This Is Not Love's Offering" is from *Bathing in the River of Ashes: Poems* by Shaun T. Griffin. University of Nevada Press, 1999.

Thanks also to Rodolfo Hernando for his poem, "Zopilotes," which appears here in Spanish from *Memoriales*, San José: Editorial Costa Rica, 2003, and in translation as "Buzzards."

When you hear a crow
in winter, it wants rain.

—anonymous

for the scavengers

THE FALLEN NATURALIST

Peacock

The breath of ten she-men
floating in blue-green robes.

First Light, Collioure

The birds motion to stars
come down, come down.

A trumpeter swan
divines the light.

A faint crescent
tears at the horizon.

Far away, Icarus climbs
from his wooden bed.

The ritual migration
from particle to animal.

And the waning dark
lifts to wings.

Starlings under Snow

           For days
the twitch of wings
       among the needles, weaving
grass, reed, and twig atop
the fork of limbs.

         Far from sky
every breath of nest
     a floating cup for eggs,
now woke to heavy silence
         of June snow.

      The wet branches bent
to plow, no ants trailing
      the tether of limbs. Soon
the melting white snapped
from cone to cone

      and each thread
       sorely gathered
fell to earth like stone.
And the nest-makers
      may never return.

The Blue Heron at First Light

for J.

Twice you folded the melancholy light
with wings: once for my brother, once
for the world that will not speak to him.

The tender piers of Wilmington
beguiled the ocean dark; still you dared
to nest amidst the rotting wood.

We boys crept the planks to a tapered bill
that slowly wheezed the awkward chill.
My dear, bony kin, pierced the distance

between bird and water for seconds
till your pewter tips broke for cover
to glide the Spartan masts. When he

reached for wings a second time,
you moved as if a needle of the night
to lift the solitary beak to sky.

He never turned to raid the egg at rest.
The channel wedged the half of you
to crown the isle of wood: his flesh

wingless and yours, nearly weightless
save the residue of gray feathers
that strangely came to comfort him.

If there were but station or friend
he would strike like a predator to feed,
yet moments after your great carriage

rose, I saw him lose at first light
the will to fly, even as the sun
came to cradle the reeds of your skin.

The Dance of the Evening Grosbeaks

for Daniel J. Griffin, 1929-1995

With white cones and matching shields,
the grosbeaks dart a skeleton elm
like thieves, not knowing
spring holds their smoky backs
like a father holds a son:

loose but for fingers turned to ribs—
and their spiny feet curl to branches
that list the fence. It is near daylight
and I, reeling from loss, list too,
but they squawk the terrace thrice

and weave a great mask sailing high.
Below the elm, a Scotch pine, planted
for the stoic climb from stone. To tame
the sky I seed a small tradition of leaves
or needles where feathers may light.

My father fled this earth and tomorrow
my hands will work the frozen ground.
And the grosbeaks, wherever they will,
skim the providence of winter
to tease the buds from sleep.

The Last Songbird on Malta

for Doc, for the Malta
songbirds hunted for sport

All night, the glorious footsteps of rain
on Spanish tiles, the persistent reminder
of moisture from sky. In the arid hill
country of France, the night damp
came as cold messenger.
Then daylight. We opened
the shutters to a sparrow
in the eucalyptus.

*I heard
the last songbird on Malta, broken
from the melodious chant of wings.
And how we must survive
"the immaculate voice of extinction."
I am wont to recreate its sound,
the empty grief before light.*

Even carrier pigeons, sworn in their flock,
mark the vines with hope.
But for the three sparrows
in the wisteria at St. Julians, the chatter
soars from memory. Not theirs, but kin
splintered by errant island shells.
And now the bird mending, the tireless
restraint to stay alive.

Who must sing
for the last of their tribe?
The echo of starvation
regards a wing as friend of hunger.
On the island of stone and flowers,
the songbird heeds the infinite cry:
leave me this wing of peace.

The Great Horned Owl at the Petroglyphs

Straight as the stony men
who flank the gorge, the horned owl
turns to reach them. No idle warrior,
ribbons of white and brown
drape wings, and the terrible eyes,
two tufts on the wind.

There is no need for darkness:
the cry of paleolithic man
scrapes the canyon, and the nocturnal one
stalks his sadness. He remains
hunched in the hollow
of wings and leaves.

The stick men look on, not yet
scrubbed from volcanic tuff.
The horned owl squints
the aperture of fences and
buckshot tin. There can be no
freedom from arrows

where each regards
the symbols of lost kin. Floating
in the notch of horns,
two legs almost run
to an outcropping
washed with the dung of eagles.

Marváo

The crisp morning sun,
the clatter of sparrows at the window.
               Under heavy blankets
sleep came at last. Through
stone porticos, two centuries of hands
           move the darkness.
Before, nothing but stars
and roosters to page the dawn.

This is how we travel: by twists
          of light, from border
to face, looking for filament,
momentary waking
in the long train to another land.

And finally surrender
to the myriad declarations
         of toilets, taxis, and temples.

All things move the heavy
        breath of loss.

What do we know?
        Sun restores. Sparrows
rake with song and soiled speech
empties to silence.

Mourning Dove

I

Four mountain bluebirds
shrieked from pine—
raised and drilled
bough to cone to needle

no species dance here—
it was blood
born of the last meal
brought them from sky

to grieve
the fledgling dove
pooled in feathers
at the window.

II

I shriek to watch you
fly no longer—
stubbled cage
your season for death.

Tomorrow
bitters all names
in the long sky
clawed to summer grass.

Bird you did not know
to kill
the feline dragon
in morning song.

III

Now the breath of beasts
cuts beneath my feet—
tendrils of rage
close in.

The blue wings
dart and retreat
from the ashen hole
left you—

a long note
torn from the breast
ooah-ooo-oo-oo
this June solstice.

Zopilotes

De negro severo como conviene
   al oficio de despachar la inerte
   carroña, ¡oh edecanes de la muerte!
   despreciados vigilantes de higiene.
Firmamento de asombro es su dominio
   con ángeles perlúcidos que pasan
   obligados en ambiguo designio
   donde todas las certezas se aplazan.
Acentos en el aire, alas audaces
   planeando sobre tersura de brisa
   con asidua paciencia de rapaces;
solamente hay razón para su prisa
   cuando del águila el infalible ojo
   descubre en distancias mortal despojo.

Note: this sonnet is by the Costa Rican poet, Rodolfo Hernando.

Buzzards

Dressed in severe black as befits
   the workers sent to consume inert
   and decaying flesh, oh companions of death!
   despised watchmen of cleanliness.
The frightful arc of sky is their domain,
   transparent angels compelled
   to fly a windless formation
   where all certainties are doubts.
Accents on the air, audacious wings
   gliding over the breeze, smooth
   with the diligent patience of predators;
the only reason for their haste
   when the eagle's unerring eye
   discovers at a distance, final remains.

Note: this is a translation of the preceding poem.

Resurrection

The last to leave
after magpie, vulture—

the crow rises from asphalt
to the carnival existence.
He presumes innocence
in the warm cathedral,
the catechism of the dark.

The ash of wings
stretch sky.
He masks the mercy
of strangers and sees no light
beyond his own.

If you survive
he will dispense with ceremony
caw a single plaintive note
and release you
to the highway of lingering hands.

Winter Admonitions, Christmas Day,
Skiing Mount Rose

Yesterday, the high sugar pine
tilting at sky, my eldest boy
swinging from cable beside me,

the tether of weights to pulleys
to us, and he points at the Clark's
nutcracker below, nosing the

mountain gopher to eventual
bleating darkness, in the old ratchet
game of hunger and flight,

the slivered bill will prevail over feet,
lobbing their way to tree trunk,
the earth paralyzed in snow, and my

boy says, "He's not going to make it,"
like us, I think, dithering at the pole-end
of the twentieth century,

dithering for scraps on the wood lot
where once I was a boy,
teasing rodents from their dens,

but now am only father
watching my son shave feeling
from skin to stay alive.

Hummingbird

At 12 I raised the barrel not 6 feet from eyes,
the first gun I fired, a .22 caliber,
and still in flight you twisted to earth
filled with a shell the size of your bill.

That day, years ago, I thought you dead
for all time. Now you dive the back yard peach,
wibbling and wobbling over nectar, your
greenish-blue coat lost in a fluorescent whir.

Sixty times a second you delight, and no hunter,
save the memory of boys flying the sight
of an old gun. I smell your burnt flesh
on the bough and the butt kicks my shoulder

like the one that cut you down.
For a time, I wished you never return
and the wash behind my parent's house
fold in sage. But in the clearing where you flutter

you teach me to forgive a long ago boy
when he, on a dare, pulled you from sky
and snaked blood from lime feathers.
You teach me to forgive the scar

we leave on land with wings.

Osprey on the Deschutes

They floated the green slick
    to Dillon Falls,
the current raking the canoe
down river, the shadow coiled overhead:
        a white wing atop the snag
    where the nest
        grew twig by twist.

The ancient rite of brooding
    from above, brooding
for her young who would fall
    60 feet to wings and one
    to the wild green below.

No splash, the subtle breath
    of bird, spiked with
        the fuzz of dandelions.
    The hatchling
gripped every strand of air
but none would still the fall,

only the claw of species
    rising to snick
    the rhythm of water to rocks.
At last, the obdurate mother circled—
    bone-breaker, fish hawk

predator on the wooden sky.

Woodsmoke, Wind, and the Peregrine

Woodsmoke and wind—
the peregrine fished
the house sparrow's cavity.

Torn from the muscle of daily ritual,
how small it seemed:
bone, beak, and flight.

Cold and beaded in the thresh of talons,
the wingless one
who pricked the snow with pink.

Robins in the Silver Maple

Twenty degrees and the planter blown
with snow this late March morning,

they all but scuff the bark
with a fatty spool of wings.

Each to their icy station,
I thought the howling a great

melancholy bird come to claw
the sadness from the house, but no,

it was the rust of robins,
peeling the wind with feathers,

the wind that burrows the eaves.
Rousing the boys for school, I

poke the hearth to serve the day.
If it lies cold for long,

there will be no chafing
and we will garnish wood

like the red ones who would gather
worms that steam below ground.

The Sparrow Rose

These are my sunny sisters:
the trellis of limbs and wings
that snub a mountain
of piñon and juniper,
sour buds that squeeze

from this small edge,
weaverbirds
hiding under stem
and blemished yellow buds
that wilt before they bloom.

Ode to Carmen's Chickens

from Peru to Tuesday
on the Comstock

The cock crows from Carmen's hutch,
I crow with it, happy to be back.
I stood the many fences shaking
and found no altar to redeem,
took the bushy red muezzin
and let the feathers free—
the fragile door of daylight
we must step through
to live in the desert.

There are no caracoles here.
A narwhal tusk will never poke
from the mine shafts.
Coil springs and bed frames lie penitent
before the toil of home.
The inland sea has dried, the Paiute
hunters long dead in their caves.
I mark my cave with silence,
rejoice in the absence of trickery

before the world closes
once again. And march
the veiled shawl of winter
to behold the Peruvian dust on my skin
still flaking from switchbacks
to the labyrinth of Andean stone.
I walked long to find my home.
It is here, on the porch, in deep August sun
soiled with chickens and leaves.

AVIAN HEART

Red-Tail in a Snow Field

The burnished wing,
the rusted tail
arc the sky
to wood
and earth.

How many more
cut the horizon
with flight?
Imagine
each red star
fallen to ash.

Piñon Jays

Motorcycle gang of the bird family,
Tom spits from the Chevy.
They squawk the dingy shoots of juniper,
cluster blue jackets in sappy piñon
and thrash the stumps of sage.
It wasn't fire set them free,
but the spectacle of noise
on this wrinkled mountain.
No piñon jay would nuisance
a street-side lantern.

Last winter Tom carved a reindeer
from mountain mahogany,
plucked its sticky leaves for antlers.
It may never fly from the hearth
but his wood lies in a haven of birds,
oily blue and black.
We need the noise,
Tom cracks from his shed
as they whack-whack-whack
the power pole in full dress denim.

Ezra's Crow

I

At twenty I walked the orange grove
from college reading Ezra Pound
till black from treetop came
the shrill weight of sound.
But there was no malice
to forgive, only the scented
air of hardwood and crow,
naked before the city. Audacious bird—
what snares a wing to grief?

II

Driving the tender desert home
the crows have followed
from Phelan to Pear Blossom
through a winter draw: shadow birds
anoint the wellspring of sorrow.

III

There is no flight left
to soothe its brow—
the ash of wings rise
to scuttle the abiding light
of late November. If crow
could tell, it would be in pictographs
like Pound, the hazel sky bent
to marrow, with scant food to follow.

IV

Fickle in flight,
hearsay on the wind,
if it could tell the bolt
of feathers, my eyes
would recoil at such red:
beak that scowls to gullet
is surely huff to weaker kin.
If not, what other death
such a heinous cry portends?

V

All the way home cheated by absence,
Ezra gone like the orange wood,
the crow not yet flown.
A silence sings to bone.
No tally of wings
will presume innocence
for crow, for poet.
At this altitude the feral quill has fallen.

The Goldfinches at Mid-Morning

Here in the firelight of pine sun,
of black oak sun, more yellow
than canary breasts, came four—

timid first, then beating the black
dam of thistle and what all my grand-
mother found at the drug store—

I read the lawless news of Andrea,
a single mother who danced
the winded caves of Sacramento

bars to feed a child. And twisted
with the she-mother preening:
would I finger a twenty

for her fiery dream of law school?
Tufted in lace, her lines a ritual
for the sleeper train to Syracuse,

for the daughter she must leave
to fight the nest of failure.
And will the goldfinches find her

knocking bargains from the dime store
when she is but a stranger
in the tangled light of a city?

When the Buttons Leave for School

When buttons swing for the door,
when boys but corner the pole
and pinch the clouds to school,

when free on feet, they swagger
the ditches, ducking and twitching
like a covey of quail,

when the mighty shadow of legs
boils to steps,
they hook the hole in the road

dreaming the playground
has fallen to popsicles
that cross the lips with icy red.

And when the talons
pounce the last to leave,
oh smallest bird, my child,

you will skip to sage
and fire a magical lance
good-bye. And huddle

with numbers and letters
and wasted events that crook
the wings to the cornice of age.

The Snowy Egret Slough

Father, you followed me to Chile.
Today, in the slough, the snowy egret
still as rice, waiting for shadow,

for insect to glaze the surface of water,
the crustacean fingers below gray sky
and my family plods behind me,

a ruddy duck at best, no grace
in my standing as you pierce
the inlet with each, pointed print,

a lingering memory of us
muddled in the shallows, my kin
too little to understand

we forget our fathers to free them,
until the river surges, narrowly
gorged from rock in Isla Negra,

the plover birds etch the silt,
and I wade the smoky bottom
but cannot follow: your white

powder wings lift to sky—
my shadow family falls to mist, and I
start the river home without you.

This Is Not Love's Offering

for a child in the Sudan

Having little to do with Eros
the vulture cranes to feed:
the child of famine recedes
to skin, and the black bird inches
to pierce the web of pulse
playing out on the desert floor.

The bird may not know
the breath of a child, may
be unfamiliar with his sighing.
But soon the two will merge
to prey upon the living
in a photograph.

When the child wakes
to another world, solemn
with the feathers of struggle,
there will be no eyes to receive him,
no camera to record. He will lie
as he was, in the kingdom of birds.

Wood Mouse

not quite winter solstice

What sacrificial offering
brought us to hunger
in the frosted light?

A wood mouse
jerked to the road.
On the horizon, the pointed

bird stands. I stop
to fill her eyes with mine:
the scripture we chant to survive.

Nocturnal, banded, and flush
with snow feathers, she stalls,
the prey three hours dead.

Cold, lifeless red
on the back of this mountain:
skeletal, tawdry death

drew us to this place
and I am no less a wing
thrashing flesh to ground.

Releasing Sparrows at the Buddhist Temple

for Stephen Shu-Ning Liu

For 20 bäht, the bird woman opens the cage,
releases six sparrows to the saffron light
and chants, *Good luck will follow all your days.*

I thought of you in Hainan, paying cents
to free a snowy egret from the farmer's hatchet,
the farmer who shook in disbelief, *Stupid man*—

but how could he know your grandfather
was a yellow crane released to the long ago
fiction of home, and you, caged in the gilded temple

of the desert, loose all wings in your path
to wake with family and teach a literature
so few will read. And hasn't it always been hard

for birds, and some would say, for us?
You fool the temple dwellers, cross the Yangtze
to freedom, then light on foreign land,

the yellow crane no one understands.
And the flight begins: beneath the scurvy
of survival, each day a piece of luck.

Pigeon

Graceless rooftop squatter
you cobble a walk from feathers,

churn the underbrush of cities,
mad for the corn that never falls.

What sends you, feckless bird,
nearer to gray than black,

to preen with those once fed,
the ordinary luxury of plump?

Even as I navigate the curve
of your hundred rueful bodies,

a white one flitters
the great broom of you to feed.

Yoking the Wing with Rose Hips

Sunday, almost a day for smoky birds
to buttress a wild rose. They sluice sound
from the winter spines, the warbling of air
against the reeds. Not Trane, not Bird,
but fluted angels who finger feet
under wings. The scuttling gray
half moons in the trees
and tree woods below them.
Back of their heads, a teardrop
bobs the eternal path to food, a fool's cross
in the road. The darkling shape
snaps from bird to bird and they scramble
as if to choke the peregrine from sky. He dives
at the bunching quail— not wind beneath them
but the sonic halo of death
coming to yoke the wing with rose hips.

In church my sons rattle cheeks to brass
and I think, not Trane, not Bird
but soon tears swamp my lids—
the hawkish cry of father
echoing the pews. I have not made
a pine bed on which to lie;
their whistling valves must do.
Who is the smokier kin,
those feet turned to barbs
or two boys burning notes
from a balcony? Neither I say.
Both are balanced, flesh to wind.

Note: the nicknames reference jazz greats John Coltrane and Charlie "Bird"
Parker.

Emerald Lake

Campfire, cook stove, cold mountain.
Not far from Han Shan, my boys and I
on a glacial cirque, the youngest
twitching the Ugly Stik, the sacred
golden trout inches below the surface.

On what green splinters do we lay our lives?
Pine bough, alpine lake, stumpy moon.
Overhead, a falcon sweeps sky and
last night, the haunting wings
in our camp— was he wounded or hiding?

I reason with the marks of work and men
most of the year, but today, smoke-filled
and arguably, the happiest I've been, relinquish
my stern hold on things and clutter the lake
with my bones, the three of us, cold naked stones.

Walking the Gray Light Home

for Barbara

Walking the gray light home
the Mexican freetail bats
skitter the river gorge:
Austin under the apron of rain.

Survivors, I thought,
the phantom birds who breach
the night with insect travel, lay waste
to the melancholy light.

Weary and long at dinner
we drank warm beer in the quiet.
A last thread tore your nephew
from the street to silence.

Suspended in the runway damp
you hitched a plane to Kalamazoo
with coffee and black toast,
the cold apron of family calling.

No room for the monotone good-bye,
I watched you arc the river of black skin
pulled from wing to solemn wing,
little girl gone to some other wind.

Postcard to Wally Easterly From Here
in the Loneliest Town on Highway 50

Nevada unfolds
       to snow cloud
       barnacle ridge
       still water
       inked with dry mountains.

All day the burrowing
       sky eats the last
       hours of April.

Mile-markers cut the road edge:
       white flags
       with no country to bear
       save greasewood and alkaline flats.

We swim the desert's black skin
       a highway of turtles
       turned belly up,
       the milky stomachs
       vulnerable to flesh-eating birds.

What I would give
       for a raven on my chest.

Waking from the Charcoal Dark

for A.

The birdhouse beckons
              but no bird will nest
       "at blackberrying time"
 the pine cone swings from twine
          girded with peanut butter and sesame seed
              for winds yet to blow
the old wooded sky crowds to comfort
              these few hours Sunday morning
       before the crack of an ax
all breath hinged on a tree limb
       and my son flies a string of leaves
to the ground.

A phone call from the prison cell
       empties the room: the web begins
       to unravel. They too were boys.

Last night in the broken dark
       the flashing of a friend
stretchered from helicopter to hospital
and this morning every line I read
       from a fine Vermont poet
seems the horned owl blinking
       at the devious clotting
   of charlatans holding forth
and I cannot pretend— let them pronounce
the death of dreams. I must get on with my life.

The sun rides the juniper
         harnessed with silver berries
the locust spines
     pierce flesh to remind:
morning has come. Let them fiddle
the four corners of doom. I must thread
the road with blackberries, worm the apples
and close my fingers in soil, this before breakfast
     on Sunday morning.

The Loons on Walker Lake

Already, you know this story will end
in the glands of waterfowl
digging the metallic river.

Now one hundred years gone,
the stamp mill's dirge
is a flute beneath the silt.

The unlucky loon
volunteers nothing from shore
and I remember Twain

who likened us to loons
in the saline brine
before the mines went down

this river become lake
to loons with no surface
for the patina of gold.

The Seagull Chicks at Berlenga

Hundreds and hundreds wobble the rock,
beak and burrow under wings,
the dirty feathers not yet flown

and wonder the spectacle of human feet
twice their size. Hundreds and more
who chirrup the hungry notes.

There cannot be sardines to answer.
Caprice will teach flight's first lesson:
you sky, you water. If they return

to mother's milky plumage,
she will spite them. There is no room
on this molting island for diving kin,

the motion of waves a cage
for the razor light of gills
slipping the garden of stone.

The Grey Elliot Riff

Not the whiskered breath of Umatilla
        scudding the range
or the foggy river out your door
but the way you swam Hopkins
        and cummings, upstream
"mud-luscious" to the floor.

Not the wrinkled print of stilt
        in the Stan Field slough
or the cowbirds tented on the post
but the soft flush of Monica
        sailing from Cimmiyotti's
that late ride to the bar.

Not the pounding of pileated
        pecker on the musty volumes
or writers wintered in the shed
but the way you closed the spring
        to college after so long
a learned life in its maw.

Not the dragon magpies piercing
        the feckless wheat
or the inky halo from a plow
but a drift on the John Day
        with ample repose—
king of the sanded bar

lilting in a poem by the shore.

Costa Brava

Woke early to the sound of *sorsal*,
picaflor, and *gaviota* marking sky,
a child peeing in the beer garden,
a husky yelping at the stray on the wall
and deep in our den, the children
wicking the cold round their necks.

They sleep in the shadow of flowers
at their windows. All night
I dreamt of places gone to seed
from work, stones, and belief.
I could bring myself to none of them
on the long bone of Chilean shoreline.

I am no more than hummingbird
shrieking that copper bill at the glass,
the dove-like *sorsal* probing shrubs
and endless gulls serving the remainder of sky.
I am a flower lance nested with kin
in a house above the sea.

City of Gray

at the church of the catacombs, Lima

The city of gray slows to sun,
the apricot buildings peel to stone.
Pigeons swarm the square like children

and tossing kernels to feed them
I think of the Quechua proverb:
Ama suwa, ama llulla, ama q'ella—

don't steal, don't lie, don't laze.
If such wisdom could exist
my mouth would tarnish

with the telling, but the child
and the pigeon do not hide:
the fog has curled to let them fly.

Mouette

for Gladys

Five years since I topped those trees
and still your voice shimmies the ladder:
You're too high, the chainsaw jerking
overhead, sweat fogging the goggles.

Bony in the Sierra foothills, the juniper
tendrils you stretched to family, *mouette,*
seagull of the Belgian underground,
circling your brood in the driveway.

Now the ordinary drizzle of loss: no voice
to chant the dust from limbs, no cloth
to stir the webs from eaves, no woman
to tender the winnowing arms.

We lip the animal music on your once-deck:
goldfinches whiskered in thistle,
a hummingbird slurring sugar water,
the raccoon nosing the ash can. He sniffs

for the tail of your broom in the garden,
the last rose drowning in sunlight.

October Hunting

I woke to birds falling numb
on this island home
where bougainvillea tints to orange
and hibiscus tips from stone
to shelter the fledgling wing.
And still the timorous whistle
of sparrows arcing the street,
the unhunted hands of neighbors
playing birdsong on phonographs
to gather them in gunless yards,
all restless meaning put aside
to witness Sunday buckshot,
each blunt note a telegram across the isle
and I will do no more than leave
this place to memory, my handcart
filled with fallen names—
like the silent before me,
I christen the tongue with shame.

Requiem for an Artist

for T.

In the shed, a merlin
        spread wing to wing. Soft
pine, the grain on which
        it dries. Out of the corner
the eye unfolds to neck,
        slack for what will suffer
the winter work of mites,
        the small storm of mouths
who dance flesh from him
        splayed over the bench,
a winged rosary for the
        buckshot spirit within.

How do we pray thee?
        Feather, creel, harness
to a weather not known?
        No earthen reply for wings.
Only wind that rides
        the bluest of embers
down-chimney to score
        the dark with rage.
Oh solemn one, you slip
        the jagged *bik-bik*
of flight with stripes
        of prodigal, banded light.

May in the Saddle atop Jumbo Grade

Camas lily, lupine, phlox—
to whom do I pray
at this crimson altar
on high Sierra wind?

A meadowlark echoes
and not one to listen.
The teardrop manes
of four mustangs

beseech the smoking city:
all grave wishes
let loose to dust
that one of us may attend

this ceremony.

When the Wings Came Down

autumnal equinox: Topaz Lake

Yesterday, with the boat no longer sport
but a wedge to carve the topaz lake,
I nearly sliced a western grebe.

When I climbed the stern to family,
my boys yelled, "You killed him!"
but the bird shot through,

left me to glide the water
unnaturally still for that instant
when the skag of ski

routed the surface to find
his image darting the wrinkles
of my blue flesh and I freed

my hands of the rope
to skim the wake of dying
leaves and failing insects

that first fall day
when the wings came down.

Tanager

For seven years you have lived in my wood,
and twice seven before that idle moment
the first yellow wing sloped to pine,
incredulous then at such radiant flight,
I fled the hope of seeing you again.

Were it mine to choose, I would name
you fireweed, or tanager, or woman,
but it is not mine. You have many
names and like the bird so long ago flown,
they have aged into colors not yet known—

colors you would feather
if it were flight and not my hand
embraced so young. Now I ring
the forest with memory and see her only
thrice these waning years:

the spectral bird having flushed
the two of us from our dens
to mate and moan and marry
the distal silence when each could send
a wing to sweep the widening door.

Not as messenger did she come,
but woman to spring the waiting flesh.
How is it a pastel bird can wince
the years to rest, and so doing,
wake the waiting flesh? She can.

On the Porch

The sparrows are racketing
      high in the feeder
and I am low in the saddle
      of a book, not one
but many wings tethered to seed.

Late Harvest without Moon

Nothing is over
all limbs bob, the piñon jay
corks three fat apples.

The Ornithologist's Prayer

Neruda would not have named you,

       Vallejo gone mad before weeping a lie

and I

       will not give breath to the rhetorical end

                       in sight:

no bird shall repair

       to the coded history

of wings,

            etch the skeletal

       mosaic of time

          with its silence.

Afterword: Seven Years

Seven years after starting on this book a western meadowlark flew into my yard. Unlike the first meeting when I heard a godless, terror-shrieking from the bird, this one released such melody I thought it unknown and resonant. Looking up to the top of the blue spruce, the yellow breast crowned with black stripes sang as if to announce a closing, and paradoxically for this beginner, a new span of years for wing watching.

My cat caught that long ago meadowlark and holding its pierced torso in my hands, I was powerless to save it. Now the bird sings again from a spruce shoot, quickening me to music under the autumn sky.

Years later we found a tapered pine root on Wildhorse Island, and poked it in the yard for a perch, where the noisy piñon jay, the robin, and the house sparrow come to rest. The minions of neglect in the bird world drop to bathe in a bath beyond my window. The songbird remains. I was his fluted understudy for seven years. Now I release these voices to wind. From the moment I began, my learned host came naturally which, if my hands could touch, would nevertheless, speed to flight.

Yesterday, South African Kevin Carter was remembered for his photograph of a vulture waiting to feed on a child too weak to walk to the food that would save him. Mr. Carter, having come to the Sudan to save his own life as a photographer, shot the picture, pushed the bird from the child and got him to the rescue station. Three months later, while on another assignment, his best friend, a journalist, was killed. Overcome with grief, Mr. Carter took his own life. I would not find this out until seven years after seeing the photograph that won him the Pulitzer Prize. These events mark us with wings, and I am left in thrall to their wisdom.

At least three volumes, but more I know, helped me to finish this collection: Charles Bergman's *Wild Echoes*, Leonard Nathan's *Diary of a Left-Handed Bird Watcher*, and Robert Leonard Reid's *Mountains of the Great Blue Dream*. Which hand do I hold out to them: the one of regret for not having known of their countenance, or the grateful palm for pushing me to think farther and longer about so common a threshold as flight. Coming to the end of a century of mechanized travel the lowly cormorant, the frigate bird, and the "worthless coot" seem no less a miracle than tears edging from cheeks, and I, ever more a witness to their silent evolution.

S.T.G.

Shaun Griffin is the author of four books of poetry, including Bathing in the River of Ashes (University of Nevada Press, 1999) and Snowmelt (Black Rock Press, 1994); has edited two literature anthologies, Desert Wood: An Anthology of Nevada Poets (1991) and The River Underground: An Anthology of Nevada Fiction (2001); and has contributed to numerous anthologies, journals, and magazines. In 1995 he received the Governor's Award for Excellence in the Arts; in 2006 he received the Rosemary MacMillan Award for Lifetime Achievement in Art from the Sierra Arts Foundation.

He is the co-founder and director of Community Chest, a non-profit social justice agency serving children and families in northwestern Nevada and former founding director of the state's homeless education office. He teaches poetry as a volunteer at Northern Nevada Correctional Center, participates in poetry programs in Nevada schools, and has taught psychology and creative writing at Western Nevada College. Mr. Griffin holds a B.A. in psychology and an M.S. in counseling from California State University, Fullerton. He lives in Virginia City with his wife Deborah and has two sons, Nevada and Cody.

Colophon

Designed and produced by Robert Blesse at the Black Rock Press,
Department of Art, School of the Arts, University of Nevada, Reno.
The font is Centaur, which was designed by Bruce Rogers in 1914,
based on the fifteenth century Renaissance roman typefaces
of Nicholas Jenson. Its corresponding italic is Arrighi,
designed by Frederic Warde in 1925, based on
Ludovico Arrighi's chancery font, Venice, 1520.
Printed by BookMobile, Minneapolis.

BLACK ROCK PRESS